MW01686888

Words of Inspiration, Hope and Encouragement from the Father's Heart

HIS *Love* REVEALED

Mardy Hodgkinson

HIS LOVE REVEALED

ISBN: 978-1-77069-794-2

Word Alive Press
131 Cordite Road, Winnipeg, MB R3W 1S1
www.wordalivepress.ca

WORD ALIVE PRESS
Just Write!

Cataloguing in Publication may be obtained through Library and Archives Canada

I dedicate this book to you
As a gift from God – His love is true.......

He's Waiting for You

You're Never Alone

Love One to Another

Growing Up

God Sees and Hears

His Healing Love

His Gift–Your Freedom

Acknowledgements

I give my heartfelt thanks and appreciation to my daughter, Joan Gericke, my daughter-in-law, Carol Hodgkinson, and my grandaughter, Krista Richens for their constant encouragement, and hours devoted to the proofreading, typing, and assistance given resulting in the publishing of this book. I am so very grateful, also, to many other family members and friends for their positive and encouraging comments and responses to the gift of these verses. Without your help and encouragement, this book would not have come into being...

In His precious love,
Mardy Hodgkinson

I thank my God, as He gave to me
Word upon word to plant His seed
That it might be scattered around the world
And for those who read it and trust His word
This seed will grow and you will see
His love and power will always be
And I send my love with His to share
To let you know I really care
For in these days of dark distress
Only His love can give you rest
Whoever you are -- whatever you do
My prayers, though silent, are covering you

He's Waiting for You

My Old Friend Bill

I have a story to tell and this story is true
It's about an old man and his mare named
Sue
It's been tucked away in my memories for
years
And I can't tell it now without shedding some
tears
We lived in the country, and down the hill
Lived a funny old man whose name was Bill
He lived alone on a very large farm
We kids thought him crazy, but he meant no
harm
He spent most of his time just cleaning the
barn
He wore funny old clothes, and so we would
tease
A heavy plaid coat down past his knees
He said it protected him from the cold winter
breeze
Black rubber boots that squeaked when he
walked
And a hat that was shredded from the brim
to the top
Gloves that made us wonder
how they kept his hands warm

For they were full of holes and needed to be darned
We'd laugh, but he'd explain:
"It's 'cause I have no yarn"
Now I must tell you more about this friend of mine
He loved to drink homemade dandelion wine
We helped him pick many a pail of flowers
For a penny or two we would pick for hours
When he drank his wine he would head for town
And, except for his friend, he would never be found
It's hard to believe but the story is true
His wonderful friend was an old mare named Sue
He would hitch up his wagon
and take off six miles to town
Old Sue knew the way and Bill would be found
Lying flat in the wagon, drunk as could be
It looked so strange for people to see
A horse drawing a wagon walking miles alone
Bringing back Bill once again safely home
She would stand at the gate,
and a neighbour would say

"Old Sue has brought Bill home again today"
They would open the gate at the top of the hill
Until old Sue was in, then they'd take care of Bill
Leaving him to sleep off the dandelion wine
And thanking Sue for bringing him home one more time
Now the old man died one day in his shack
And as kids, we cried, and wanted him back
We were sorry we laughed at the clothes that he wore
And the stories he told that we thought were a bore
No reason to pick dandelions anymore
But the saddest thing was yet to come
And we all knew it had to be done
But as kids we didn't know what to do
How could we tell his best friend, Sue?
Do horses cry, or wonder why
Their very best friend doesn't come anymore?
Will she just keep watching the old barn door?
Somehow I thought, "Yes, she always will
Be sadly watching and waiting for her old friend Bill"

....

Now, like God, Sue was just faithful and true
And her love for old Bill was all she knew
Her desire to be with and protect her best friend
Is the love I've come to know that will never end
From God who doesn't judge by the clothes we wear
The way we talk or the style of our hair
He sees our heart and understands
And simply wants us to take His hand
And walk through the journey of life together
So that in the end we can be with Him forever
And as for old Sue, she'll join him again
In heaven so blessed and free from all pain
For there's a place in heaven for animals to roam
In peace and joy – their eternal home

Back Home

I stood at the top of the mountain
And looked down to the valley below
I saw the most beautiful flowers,
But I was standing in the snow
I watched an eagle soaring
Carried by a soft blowing wind
I saw God in all His glory
And I raised my arms to sing
But seeing the wonder of His splendour
Left no words to say,
So while letting silent tears roll down
With thankfulness I did pray:
"Oh, God, forgive me, for I didn't see
How far from You I had strayed,
And in Your gentle, loving way
You brought me back home today"

If There's A Place

If there's a place our God hasn't forsaken
Where sin and evil haven't been taken
If there's a valley all green with clover
With daisies from sunshine brimming over
If there's a stream filled with trout
That a fisherman can brag about
A mountain high to shield the night
From any harm, and from all fright
A place to lay my weary head
At the end of the day then let it be said
That this be heaven

Race For Life

We try so hard in life to win the race
But fall apart when we come in second place
Didn't we know when we started out
Our chances for winning always carried a doubt
For so often in our race for life
We look for love, but find only strife
Yet there is a promise if you will just trust
In the end you will win, but to believe is a must
Life can be an obstacle course, so before you begin
Give God your dreams, surrender all to Him
Don't lay out the plans thinking that's how it will be
But live one day at a time letting Him help you to see
That though the sun may not shine today
He's there in your darkness to light the way
He's there to help you, and you will overcome
The race for life is not over – it's really just begun

The Highway

Life is a highway – there's really no end
When I think I have made it, there comes another bend
Did I start out with a map in my hand?
Did I see the mountains, the valleys, the sand?
Did I know of the cold in the night or the heat of the day?
Did I heed all the signs that showed me the way?
No, I just kept going even when I knew
The signs said "danger" – I thought I'd get through
I'm still on the highway and wondering where
And when it will end and I'll finally be there
If this is my life, should I just stop?
No, I must keep going for it's just what I thought
I've come a long way, but I'll reach the top
Will I read the last sign, or will I care
If at the end of the highway nobody's there?
No, I'll surrender and know in the end
My travels are over –
I'm with my best friend

To Start Again

I came looking for you today
You were trying to hide, then I heard you say:
"Forgive me, Lord – I went astray
I'm Your lost sheep and afraid to say
That I fell again – I know it's wrong
I fell into temptation – sometimes it's so strong
I feel ashamed and want to hide
As only time may turn the tide
But I know there's really no place to go
That You won't see – that You won't know"
I listened and again I heard you say:
"God, forgive me - I have fallen away"
But you know I love you just the same
I heard you when you called My name
I'll always forgive – you can start again…
My love for you is always the same

The Way, The Truth, and The Life

When I reach out my hand to others
It is not to take – it's to give
And when I say: "God is waiting for you"
It is not to die – but to live
He holds the plan for your future
And if only we'll give Him His way
We won't have all the sorrow
We seem to have from day to day
When we are unable to find our way
And feel so lost and lonely
And think we've gone astray
Stop everything for a moment
And listen to Him say
"My child, the cares that you are carrying
I'm here to take away
Trust Me to have the answers
When you feel so full of strife
And remember what I promised
I am the Way, the Truth, and the Life"

Open the Door

To you who have stumbled and fallen away
And who feel so guilty – you can't even pray
You have heard of a God who forgives every day
But you haven't yet met Him and don't know what to say
You're so afraid He'll say: "Guilty" – and punish you
So you really don't know what you can do
You just feel so guilty and full of shame
But your heart is hurting and wants to change
This letter is from God and addressed to your name
Open it and read it – you'll never be the same:
"My child, don't listen to what others may say
I've come to love and protect you in every way
You'll know a love you have not yet known
A Father you can trust, and truly call your own

Just open your heart and let Me come in
And I'll forgive and forget your every sin
I'll wait at the door that's been shut
for so long
And forgive all those things
you thought were wrong
And turn on the light and give you more
Than you've ever dreamed of having before
I'm the answer to what you've been looking
for
All you have to do is open the door"

You're Never Alone

God's Tears of Love

As I walked alone in the rain today
In a quiet moment I heard God say:
"The tears I'm crying – you call them 'rain' –
Are My tears of sorrow, for I cry in vain
I miss My children – they have strayed away
But I keep calling them every day
My heart is broken as I see them leave
If only they knew how deeply I grieve
I gave to them My only Son
To show them all that He is the One
To prove My love if they would believe
All they need do is trust and receive
I've prepared them a home – and this could be
Where they could spend eternity
If only they'd listen and heed My call
My arms are open to give them all
That I have promised – if they would only see
How much I want them to live with Me"

My Mom's Last Day

She opened her eyes but she couldn't see
She listened but she couldn't hear
She moved her lips but she couldn't talk
She moved her legs but she couldn't walk
Then, with tears she sank into deep despair
When an angel whispered: "You'll soon be there"
Then she took her hand and I heard her sing
"She's going home, she's going home
Her way is prepared right to the throne
Where there's singing and dancing, joy and peace
And so much love it will never cease"
So I closed my eyes and I thought a prayer
For I knew her Jesus was waiting there
Oh what peace filled my heart
And for her last journey, she was ready to start
For I knew in my spirit when she took her last breath
She would always be living, she would never know death

The Rainbow

I reached up and touched the rainbow
And I heard it say:
"Hold tight to my every colour –
They will get you through today
Don't look at the clouds around me
They will lie to you again
And only try to convince you
Of all your sin and shame
But God painted for you this rainbow
And in colour He wrote your name
Look for me, and remember
I will always be the same
He'll paint for you a rainbow of love
And until you see me again
Just keep looking up and know
I will always follow the rain..."

The Birds

I sit at my window alone
Looking out at the sky above
And I see such wonderful things,
Especially the birds that I love
I ask God every morning
To give me a reason to live
And He answers my every longing
When I see the gifts that He gives
The birds are so very special
And when I hear them sing
My heart just lifts in wonder
At the music they do bring
I look at the beautiful sunrise
Announcing the coming of day
And I no longer feel so lonely
Knowing God is with me to stay
And like the birds I'm watching
That fly so high above
I'll find my reason for living,
As I sit here embraced in His love

As He talks to me each morning
I listen to hear Him say:
"My gift to you – the birds you love
Are a sign from Me today
That when I come to take you home
Safe within My arms of love,
You, too, will fly as they do now
So free, so far above"

Life's Challenges

Life is a challenge we all have to share
Look for the answers, they're always there
Don't go down in life's defeat
The answers could be in someone you'll meet
Maybe today, maybe tomorrow
God will send someone to lift your sorrow
Don't give up and think you have failed
Think of Jesus and how He was nailed
They thought He was finished, His life had an end
But our struggles and pain, He took them to mend
And gave His life freely for us to share
The challenges of life that, without Him, we can't bear

Your Path

Your path will be sprinkled with laughter and tears
And sometimes sadness – sometimes fears
There will be times when you don't understand
This is when you take His hand
The path will look brighter than it did before
And you'll know you've found what you're looking for
The trials you thought would never mend
You leave behind and walk on to the end
And you'll find the peace you've been looking for
That you couldn't find on your walk before
You're on the same path, but there was a bend
Now you're hand-in-hand with Jesus, your best friend

His Hand

When the storms of life engulf me
And I don't know where to turn
I sit quietly and listen
And my thoughts become more firm
I feel a deep, deep stirring
And it rises ever up
Until I cannot hold it
And it overflows my cup
Then the storm that held me
Lets go, and I am free
And I remember whose hand I'm holding
And I slip down upon my knees

He's Always Near

Never, never on my own
Never, never all alone
Just knowing that You care
Knowing You are everywhere
Just waiting with a guiding hand
We don't have to understand
Just trust His love for us to see
His guiding light to set man free
The still, small voice we can hear
To know for certain He's always near
Take His hand and be set free

Every Step of the Way

As you walk through the valley of tears
Hold tight to My hand
And My love will be greater than all your fears
I won't let you go
I'm with you to stay
To help you and love you
Every step of the way
I know your past
I know your future
I know the heart of every creature
Don't listen to those who say I don't care
I'm waiting to help you climb the stairs
I'm reaching down to draw you near
So don't give up, I'm always here
My love is stronger than the stairs you climb
I died for you, and now you're Mine
Love, Jesus

If I Could Take Your Burden

If I could take your burden
And know it would set you free
I'd gladly open up my arms
And hope that this would be
The answer to your problems
But I know this wouldn't do
For we each have our cross to bear
And each must see it through

When Lonely

I cried a tear for you today –
Somehow we met along the way
I've seen your quiet look, your lonely stare,
Your eyes that held the question: "Doesn't anybody care?"
You think you're no one special –
They say you don't look well
But it's really that you're lonely
And don't know who to tell
They are all in such a hurry,
A busy life they lead
And you're so very lonely
They don't hear your biggest need –
To have someone really care
And talk awhile with you
To give the simple gift of time,
And an ear to listen to
And hear the cry within your heart:
"I'm as lonely as can be"
And so I stand beside you now,
Please talk awhile with me

We'll mix our tears of understanding
And I will freely share
How God has put you on my path
To tell you that He cares
And we could hold this memory
For many days ahead
And when again you're lonely
Remember what He said

I Saw You In My Prayer Today

I saw you in my prayer today –
God holding you in His arms
And then I heard Him say,
"The cares that you are carrying
I'm here to take away
To tell you how I love you
And My love will always be
And what you cannot find in others
You will always find in Me"

Love One to Another

My Mask

Don't be fooled by the mask I wear
There's a little child buried in there –
somewhere
Love me for what you cannot see
Your touch of love could set me free
There is a story behind every look
Don't judge the cover until you've read the
book

Sing My Song

I want someone to sing my song
Someone to care when things go wrong
To take the song that's in my heart
And give my life another start
Things went wrong along the way
But I pray you'll be the one to say:
"I'll sing your song that's in your heart
The one you lost along the way
Your heart will mend and you will hear
The song you sang in yesteryear"

The Silent Word

Don't think I didn't hear you
When you looked across at me
Though not a word was spoken
You said: "I'm as lonely as I can be"
And though we're perfect strangers
For a moment we both shared
That though not a word was spoken
You knew I really cared

Glad I Came

We all need someone to love and care
And in our loneliness, our thoughts to share
Think of me and send a prayer
Call my name and I'll be there
I'll hear you whisper—I'll hear My name,
And I'll be with you, and glad I came

Seeds

The seeds that we plant along the way
Are the future for some, so watch what you
say
Will they, when they grow, blossom and show
Memories of love and a friendship that
grows?
Water them when you can each time
With love and kindness and you will find
The seeds that you planted along the way
Are still bringing blossoms to brighten their
day

Tears of Love

My tears are my expression
Of a love that hides inside
It's my way of saying: "I love you" –
So please just let me cry
Sometimes there are no words to say
And so I cry instead
And pray that God will hear my prayers
And hold the tears I've shed
I want so much to help you,
But don't know what to do
So I'll just hold you close and cry
My tears of love for you

Life

Life can be like an open wound
It heals, but leaves a scar
And it is there to remind us
Of who we really are
And yet we judge and criticize others
Forgetting that they carry, too,
The same scars to remind them
That they, too, have been hurt like you
And they wish that they could find
Someone to help ease their troubled minds
So please, if in your daily walk,
You find someone in this state
Let them know you really care
Before it is too late
Listen and let them share
The burden of their heart
Let them know God loves and cares
And that this could be their new start
To face their tomorrows
Knowing they have a friend
Who is there to listen --

And though the scars won't mend
They are there to remind us
That though the wounds may now be gone
The scars that we are carrying
Can bring a bright new song

If we can only understand that they're just
A reflection of what used to be
And take them as a blessing
Then we would clearly see
That the wounds we were carrying
God took, and we are free

Call Me Your Friend

I'm sorry you don't like the clothes that I wear –
The colour of my skin or the length of my hair
And when I stop to talk to you
The things you say – the things you do
I wish just once you would look inside
And see the things I'm trying to hide
You look so good all the time
Your clothes are the best – your shoes always shine
I know I don't fit into your ways
But I need your help for my down days
You see, I have them, and quite a few
Trying to look as folks like you
If you would befriend me, and not just pretend
It would give me a beginning instead of an end
And when my days are lonely and the clouds are grey
I'll think of you and remember
You called me 'your friend' today

To The Blind Child

I know you're blind, but this just means
that you cannot see as others see
But you can touch and feel and know
Your hands are your eyes and they will show
How God will guide them – He loves you so...
Give me your hands – He sent me today
To lay in your hands this bird, and to say:
"Touch his feathers, spread his wings,
Imagine him flying, hear him sing
Although he's flying so high and beyond
Listen and hear him as he sings his song
See his wings soaring up and away
And remember you held him in your hands
today
Your hands are a gift of God's tender love
You have held the bird that's flying above
Imagine it now seeing you down below
And dipping his wings to say hello
Reach up to the birds as your hands let you
see
And know they are there, and always will be
Ask God to send them – but then most of all
Quietly listen and hear them call

And remember you held one, then let it go
free,
Your hands were your eyes that allowed you
to see
His beautiful feathers, his wings spread out
wide,
They are flying above you, and God is their
guide"

They Sang Their Song Together

I listened to a meadowlark
And a sparrow in a tree
They sang their song together
There was no disharmony
The meadowlark so colourful
And anyone could see
The sparrow so plain in colour
But happy as can be
They sang their song together
And their music set you free –
You see there was no hatred
Nor any jealousy
They sang their song together
And made me realize
That God had given the birds to us
To enjoy and colour the skies
Not for us to question
What with human eyes we see
That one is prettier than the other
Or sings a sweeter harmony

It's not for us to judge
Or for us to criticize
But just to remember
And always realize
We, too, are all God's family
And are equal in His eyes

Little Boy Blind

Little boy blind, follow me
And I'll lead you to the sea
To open shores and lands unknown
Where no foot has trod –
Only God's seed has been sown
You will see through my eyes
The blueness of the open skies
Like you have never seen before
And know the meaning of the ocean's roar
Take my hand, don't be afraid
We'll go alone, for God has made
A wider path, a greener glade
We'll find our shelter in the shade
Where naught but animal has lain
I'll take you to a virgin land
And tell you how the world was planned
Hold tight my hand with all your might
And you'll know the day –
Not just the night

Christmas Love

My gift to you cannot be bought
Or hung upon a tree
And no one else can share it
It's just to you from me
It's: "Thank you for your understanding
And your forgiving heart
When I have said or done something
That sadly made us part"
You know I really love you
You are God's gift to me
And so my gift comes unwrapped
And cannot be hung upon a tree
But will be yours forever...I give you back
The love you so sweetly gave to me

Each Day

Face each day with a burst of love
Knowing it's a gift sent down from above
Face each task with patience and faith
Care for each soul as you run the race
For what we do each day is our testing
ground
What we do for others will only be found
When we leave this world and all its cares
And go home to Him whose love we shared
We will not find, no, not one thing
That this earth provides, nor can we bring
The things that seem so important now
They're all left behind, and when before Him
we bow
I pray that I will hear Him say:
"The love you shared with those on earth
Is all that came with you today"

I Do

Yesterday when I held you
I saw a tear in your eye
And when I asked you about it
What you said made me cry
You said: "Darling, it reminded me
As I stood there close to you
The words that we whispered
When we both said 'I do'
Yes, honey, I have them
Writen in my heart
To love and to cherish
'Til death do we part"
Just two little words
But they are so true
Our promise before God
When we said 'I do'

Why

We are born, we live, and then we die
We question the reason – we want to know
why
Just stop and remember along the way
The good times you shared and the love you
displayed
Maybe some were at their end
And needed you to be a friend
You listened and held them and dried their
tears
And helped them to rise above all their fears
So in life we will wonder and often we will cry
Dear God, forgive me for asking,
For You have just told me why

In Saying Goodbye

In life's journey how often we say: "Hello"
And sometimes it's the beginning of a
friendship that grows
But, oh, the sadness and pain that we share
With all our "Goodbyes" for those whom we
care
I remember sometimes the "Goodbyes" that
I've said –
And the sorrow released through the tears
that I've shed
And I know as I sit at your side today
That the time will come when I'll have to say:
"Goodbye, my love, and leave with me
The memories we've shared, and through
them I'll see
That though the heartache is hard to bear,
I know we'll meet again somewhere
For God has provided a home above
Where together again we will share our love"

The Time Will Come For Parting

Every time we meet, sweetheart,
and softly say: "Hello", we know
That this might be the very day
that we are called to go
That this might be the last time
that we will say: "Goodbye"
So, sweetheart, I'll tell you now I'll love you
'til the day I die
The time will come for parting
and God will have His way
One will travel upward and one will have to
stay
So we must realize, sweetheart, how precious
are these times for you and me
And thank God for our time together
whenever that might be
So when we say: "Hello" –
For every moment we can spare
Let's bring heaven down to earth
for the moments we can share
And let our love surrender to God within
His loving care

Remember

I picked a rose in my garden today
And I talked to you – so far away
As I touched the petals, they heard me say:
"Remember the love we always knew
And remember I said that I'll always love you"
Even though we had to part
Remember I love you still, in my heart
And as the petals fall away
Remember the times you heard me say:
"When God calls, we'll have to part
But you were the one I called sweetheart"
Honey, if there's a garden there
And I'm sure that there must be
Pick a rose today – and let the petals flow free
And I'll be there with you
And you'll be here with me

My Love Has Found a Home

I couldn't trust you, so I pushed you away
You gave me time in many ways
You understood what I was going through
And in time I'd heal and realize I needed you
And all you were
Your patient love and quiet way
Did more for me than words can say
I was sure I would never be the same
That I would never love again
That I would have to learn to live alone
Then I found you and the love you've shown
And now my love has found a home

I Cry

I cry for what could have been
I cry for what should have been
And I cry for what is
Oh what foolish lives we live
We want to take but not to give
Even though in our hearts we know
We think we've won
But our lives have shown
We have really lost along the way
The important things of every day
They are so simple, and the gifts are free –
A hug, a smile, a word someone needs
To lift their spirit – to hear you say:
"God sends His love to you today
And I love you, too, and want to say
I'll be here for you, come what may
Ready to help you along the way"

Growing Up

A Little Girl, A Little Boy

A little girl
A little boy
A little doll
A little toy
A mud pie
A dirty face
A Sunday dress all trimmed with lace
A choo-choo train to travel the globe
A book of fairy tales untold
A work of art to win my praise
With broken crayon page on page
With a prayer each night
I build a shrine
For this boy, this girl
They're mine, all mine

On Growing Up

I heard you when you prayed
And saw the tear that filled your eye
When you said: "Oh, Lord, I'm growing up
And I'm much too big to cry
Lord, I look to others, and really love them so,
But, Lord, will You remind them
And really make them know
That they should have more patience
And show me how to grow
Then I wouldn't have the struggle
Of trying to grow up faster
And doing foolish things that bring about their laughter
And, Lord, like them, You made me, and I am special, too
Sometimes I really need them to show me what to do
But always to remember that I must be set free,
For I need their help and guidance to let me be just me"

Growing Up

Mama, growing up can be so hard to do
And every day brings something that, to me,
is new
If I broke your heart today, Mama, please
don't cry
Tomorrow I'll try harder and you'll know the
reason why
Just like the tiny sparrow, I'm learning how to
fly
And I know sometimes we don't agree
And I say things I shouldn't
But Mama, I'm just starting out to do the
things I couldn't
So Mama, guide me safely and don't let go
my hand
I know you will forgive me and I will
understand
That God has given me to you and Daddy in
His plan
And I will really thank Him and I will really try
But like the tiny sparrow I'm learning how
to fly

God Sees and Hears

God's Blessings

God's blessings come in many ways –
To the good and to the bad
To the happiest of people
And to the very sad
There are so many ways
He wants to answer you
Just listen and you'll hear Him
He'll tell you what to do
That still, small voice deep inside
We call our secret mind
It's really God speaking
So just let Him decide
He's always walking close to you
He is your perfect guide
He'll speak to you through a stranger
Or maybe your best friend
Whatever way He chooses
His blessings He will send
Sometimes in a dream
In the middle of the night
Or through His peace that overcomes you
When you watch a bird in flight
However He sends His blessings
It's with His love to you
Just wait patiently for His answers
And your prayers will all come true

My Silent Prayer

Lord, I don't come to You with fancy words
When I kneel down to pray
I wait silently and listen
To hear what You want to say:
"My child, I know your every heartache
I'm with you every day
You have come to Me this morning
Your heart is filled with pain
For those you love so very much
You bring to Me again
You don't have to say a word
Your tears for them I'm taking
I hear your silent prayer
And know your heart is aching
Just know I'm here to talk to you
And always understand
You never have to look for Me
Just don't let go My hand
I know there are so many
You want to bring to Me
Your heart is really breaking
But this need never be
I hear your silent prayer
When you don't know where to start
Just remember, I'll always listen
To the prayer that's in your heart"

My Letter to God

Dear God please forgive me – I'm so
depressed again
Please send someone to help me –
Someone who's known the pain
Someone who's known the feeling
when nothing seems to go right
And you lose your reason for living
and just can't face the night
Feeling defeat in every way –
Not wanting to live another day
Not able to smile nor even to pray
While deep inside wondering,
"Can I face another day?"
I long to be like others I see laughing and
enjoying life
But I'm locked in with tears of the memories
and the strife
Is there an answer – is there a way
To turn my nights of darkness into the light of
day?
Will I ever wake up in the morning again
To look forward to living, and not have the
pain
Of wearing a mask and trying to refrain
From the loneliness and heartache
that does return again?

To awake and feel that life has a reason
And I'm just going through another season?
God help me to know that the clouds will go
And I'll be free from the pain that I now know
That the sun will shine again once more
And with Your help I'll forget and close the door
For I know You're always with me,
and I couldn't ask for more
So God, please send an angel
who knows just what to do
To help to lift my spirit and to just depend on You
I know You really love me,
and I remember You cried too
So I'll wait for You to hold me
for I know You'll get me through

Forgiveness

Oh, Jesus, I really need You today
I'm so sorry I fell and went astray
Speak to me for I'm so lonely to hear
Please hold me close and calm my fear
Hear my heart when it calls out in prayer
And remember You said that You'd always
be there
If I have the faith of a mustard seed
You'll give me more than I'll ever need
My heart is asking – I've heeded Your call
I know You will help me and not let me fall
I long to know peace as I search everywhere
It seems to escape me, but I know You are
there
Your peace and love covers where I have
but failed
Your blood – my forgiveness – on the cross
where You were nailed

A Hug

Dear God, my heart is broken
Please hear what I have to say
That though the world is full of people
I'm so lonely and it's hard to pray
I need a hug so badly...
If You could find a way
To let me know I'm not alone
I need that hug today
Dear God, I know I'm old and withered
And unattractive, though I try,
And folks just don't know what to say
And so they pass me by
Dear God. I need to know
You'll never pass me by
I need to feel Your love with me
And know the reason why
No matter where I go
You are the only way
You were with me always
Back when I was young and gay,
And I know when others pass me by
You will always stay
Dear God, I'll just look to You
For my hug today

To heal my broken heart
And to hear You say:
"Because you are My child,
You're never old and grey
And so when others pass you by
Know I'm here to stay
You're not alone—the hug you need
I'll give you every day"

Broken Heart

I say I have a broken heart
And can't bear the pain that's there,
But I just cry in secret
For no one really cares
I wait for the pain to go away,
But deep inside I know:
"God, You're my only comfort –
There's nowhere else to go
You know my heart is broken
My only hope is You
And though I feel so empty,
I pray You'll see me through
I've cried so many tears
My eyes are never dry
And so I call again to You,
My God, please tell me why
For when I feel this pain inside
I really need to know
Can broken hearts be mended
When broken hearts don't show?
God, hold me to You closely
I need so much to know
You'll always be there with me
And my broken heart will go"

Prayer Changes Things

Prayer changes things -- this we all know
But sometimes we wonder when the changes don't show
That's God's way of saying: "Just trust and let go"
At the right time He'll open the door
And you'll see the changes you've been praying for
Yet sometimes the door closes -- the time is not now
Just wait for His answer -- He'll tell you somehow
But remember to praise Him and before Him to bow
Time is so different for His wonderful ways
So patiently trust Him 'til you hear Him say:
"The changes you prayed for are on their way"
So never give up -- just wait and pray

Help Me, Lord

Help me, Lord, to understand You
Help me to learn Your precious Word
Help me, Lord, when I'm uncertain
Help me, Lord, to find Your road
If I walk in too much boldness
Bow my head and bend my knees
Help me, Lord, to know Thy fullness
To know it's You and never me
Help me, Lord, to stretch my hand out
To my fellow man in need
Help me, Lord, oh God, please help me
That I might ever walk with Thee
Help me, Lord, to love all others
Help me, Lord, Your light to see
Help me, Lord, to just remember
Without You, where would I be?

Freedom

Oh, Father, no one ever told me
And I was too blind to see
How much You really love me
And the blessings there would be
Forgive me, Lord, forgive me
I need Your love to see
For only You complete me
Making me all You want me to be
Oh, Lord, my heart's desire
Is to love You more each day
And to hold Your hand so tightly
So that I won't lose my way
Oh, Lord, I've struggled all my life
But I just didn't see
Until You came to show me
What love can really be
You died for me – what greater love
That I could be redeemed
That in my darkest hour
Your light could shine in me
Oh, Father, I do love You so.
With tears of love and reverence
I get down on my knees
Just to thank You for Your presence

Oh, God, what could it be
That You would die upon a cross
To bear such pain and agony
And suffer so for me
You took my pain and sorrow
And have waited patiently
For me to understand and know
That I have been set free
My heart is overflowing
With my love for Thee!

Lover of My Soul

Jesus, oh my Jesus
Lover of my soul
The One who died on Calvary's cross
To heal and make me whole
Jesus, oh my Jesus
The way, the truth, the light
Help me to love You always
With all my heart and might
You suffered and You died for me
That I could live eternally
And now I ask with one last prayer
Use me to help others in their despair
That they, too, will know of Your great love
And that You're watching over us from above
Soon I know You will return
To take us Home, and I do yearn
To see Your face, Your loving face
And I will thank You for Your grace
Jesus, oh my Jesus
Lover of my soul

His Healing Love

We Cannot All Be Roses

We cannot all be roses
Loved by all and cared for each day
Some of us are weeds –
Hurt, walked on, torn up and thrown away
But this doesn't really matter
For we know that in the end
The weeds are God's natural flowers
The roses are planted by man
I think of you as such a weed
Strong, yet gentle and full of love
Though you've known hurt
This weed has blossomed
Nourished by the Father's love

The Little Child Inside

I try so hard to fit into this world
The way God had it planned
But because I feel a failure
I did let go His hand
I lost hope and all desire
Just to carry on
I feel like life's a burden
And all my dreams are gone
But that's when deep inside of me
A little child I hear:
"I'm hurting – please just let me grow
And I will make it clear
I want so much to live and love
But wonder, do you care
You've grown up and left me
Can't you come back and share
The reason you are living
I was always there"
And God wants you to remember
And always understand
He is still there waiting
And reaching out His hand
To let this little child in you
Complete His perfect plan

And when no one else will listen
To the broken heart you wear
Don't give up on Jesus
You know He's always there

The Empty House

I sat in front of the empty house
It was old, tired and worn
No one lived there anymore
And hadn't for many years
But I heard laughter still in the house
And I sat and listened in tears
The railings had long ago fallen
And there were many cracks in the stairs
And although it had been a long time ago
I felt the love from the house that was theirs
I saw him working hard as a man
Tilling the soil, working the land
And she as a wife and mother of four
Cooking and sewing and scrubbing the floor
Babies coming one at a time
Growing strong with love and secure in their minds
Now into the world their futures to find
And the man and the woman grew old and died
But the love and the laughter are still inside
And the cracked boards in the creaky old wall
Echo it still – they miss it all

And I envy those whose lives it shared
As I know in my heart they really cared
And I know they won't mind that I'm sharing
their past
For a child from this house knew a love that
lasts
When I feel sad and want to cry
And even sometimes when I want to die
I come and sit on the steps of this house
And pretend I was one of the four
Very gently I climb the stairs
And slowly open the creaky old door
The laughter gets louder than it was before
I stay awhile and become a child
And feel the love as one of the four
I think of the love that they once shared
And feel the healing presence of God
As I linger there
I walk away feeling quite secure
And forget for a while my loneliness and fear
And pretend I'd lived there in my yesteryear

Your Small World

Is your world so small
You can touch every wall
And the ceiling is falling in?
Just trust in the Lord,
He'll remove it all
Open the door and let Him come in
He will tear down the walls
Take the ceiling right off
And a new life you will begin
To know how much He really cares
And loves you, even in your sin
He'll show you how big your world really is
And He gives it all to you
Just open your eyes and realize
This world was made for you
The love, the joy, the peace of mind
Is all in knowing Him
Your world, your thoughts, all you had
Has now grown very dim
Don't look back at the fallen walls
Or the roof that lays on the floor
The only thing He left standing
Was you, Himself, and an open door

The Path

We sometimes wander off the path
Wondering what went wrong
As our world falls apart before us
And we feel we don't belong
Then God reminds us to surrender
And go back to where we began
The path is still before us
But He had a different plan
Although sometimes it's so hard for us
To really understand,
That's when He reaches out to say:
"My child, just take My hand"
Oh, Lord, I pray, please come to me
In the stillness of this night
When it seems so long and lonely,
And sometimes full of fright
Lord, it's then I really need You,
And I know that You are near
To catch the tears I'm crying
And take away my fear
And so I close my eyes once more
And wipe the tears that fall
Once again surrendering
To Your gentle, loving call

Take My Love

I loved you from the beginning
I will love you to the end
And if you'll take My love to others
This is all I ask, My friend
Take My love, take My blessing
Leave the judging all to Me
If you succeed in just My loving
You'll be all I want you to be
Just take My love, leave the changing of their lives to Me
Just let them know that the reason you love them
Is because of your love for Me
Take My love to the one who's lonely
Take My love to the crying child
Take My love and with it tell them
This is why for them I died
Oh take My love, don't keep it, share it
There are so many mournful souls
Who haven't heard just how I love them
They never will if they're not told
So take My love where e'er you wander
It will always see you through
For love is all that ever mattered
That is why I'm sending you

Take My love to all who hunger
Take My love to all who hurt
Take My love as faithful servants
It must spread throughout the earth
Take My love and you take Me
Because I am the all-in-all
Use it for your strength and courage
To pick you up when e'er you fall
Take My love and give it freely
Hearts are aching just to know
Someone loves them, really loves them
More than mortal man can show
This love is real and never ending
It's the love of Jesus all must know
So take My love where hearts need mending
Then like a river it will flow
If love is planted I will water
Come the harvest, love will grow

His Gift—
Your Freedom

Tell Me the Story

Tell me the story of the love and all the glory
Of the One who shed His blood and died for me
Tell me the story of Joseph and Mary
And the God-child who set all men free
The One who redeemed us coming back to receive us
To live with Him throughout eternity
Tell me the story, the plan of salvation
That changes our hearts and brings love to the nations
The reason for living, for loving, for giving
It's Jesus who dwells in me

Your Salvation

The key to your salvation is in the Saviour's
name
Just open up your heart to Him –
You'll never be the same
Call to Him and listen –
You'll hear Him speak your name
He'll fill you with His peace and joy,
Removing guilt and shame
You'll never be alone, or have a closer friend
Your problems you can share with Him,
He wants to help you mend
The yesterdays you thought would never go
away
The trials and temptations you thought
were here to stay
He'll pardon and forgive you,
and love you just the same
He'll never leave you or forsake you – Jesus is
His name

From the path He's laid before you,
You may slip and fall away
But in all of your tomorrows,
When you know heartache, grief or pain
He'll be there to guide you –
Take His hand and call His name
He is Jesus, the Son of God,
And will always be the same

CPSIA information can be obtained at www.ICGtesting.com
Printed in the USA
LVOW10s2144190913

353297LV00010B/152/P

9 781770 697942